Copyright © 2024 Ivonne van Dis
Illustration and design by Roos Oudt
First edition

All rights reserved.
No part of this publication may be reproduced, stored in a retrieval system, or transmitted in any form or by any means, electronic, mechanical, photocopying, recording, or otherwise, without prior written permission from the publisher. All rights reserved.

ISBN 9798339334316

For people who know they are so much more than they can imagine!

Table of Contents

Foreword	9
roles	10
I am the thinker	12
everything is energy	13
bullshitradar	15
stop it	17
on repeat	18
just being	19
simple but difficult	20
spiritual money	22
connect	24
how simple	26
criticism	28
the land beyond I don't know	30
ludo	31
words	32
reset button	34
reading glasses for thoughts	35
hacked	36
struggles	37
formula	38
dare	39

true colours	40
inner house	41
gift	43
all equal	45
vegetable garden	46
sanctuary	48
I didn't understand you before	50
freedom	51
elusive	52
ego drug	53
psycho-logical	54
part of	55
but how do I get there?	57
if then	58
labels	59
I see you	61
faking or shaking	63
truth	65
peace	67
lost	68
on repeat	69
now what?	71
I am here	72
I am experiencing	74

weeds	75
heaviness	76
I know it but...	77
holding back	80
yes but	81
no more fighting	82
thinking is not right	83
name	85
show up	87
letting go	89
desire	91
I want it now	93
but how?	94
popular to live in your head	95
almost	96
from within	98
free from	100
what you say is what you are	103
no clue	104
body to head and back	105
knowing who you are	107
frequency of words	108
one thought away	109
searching	110

self-boundary	112
disciple	114
who are you already	115
words of thanks	117
About the author	118

Foreword

We often believe that what we see is true, but what if there are more possibilities in your mind that you haven't considered yet? Because you haven't thought of them, you don't believe in them either—simple as that. Sometimes, we get trapped by our thoughts and end up overthinking brilliant ideas.

Our thinking works like a computer: what you put in is what you get out. From a young age, we are shaped by our environment and learn how life works.

As we grow older, we discover that the world outside our family is different, bringing new challenges. Eventually, most of us ask ourselves: What is the meaning of our existence? These poems serve as reading aids, helping you see your thoughts more clearly. They offer a different perspective on how we are psychologically wired and prompt you to reflect on who you are and what you are here to do. In my opinion, these are the most important questions in life.

I have searched for a long time and waited to apply the knowledge that I had within me all along.

What I've seen in practice, and experienced myself, is that we often demand too much of ourselves. We try to follow all sorts of rules and habits we've learned, and this costs us a lot of energy. The downside is that we forget who we really are and get stuck.

In this book, I share my story, which may also be your story. After all, we are all made the same way, just programmed differently. Becoming aware of this can be life-changing.

Read the poems as if they are about you and notice which new thoughts arise. You are always your own salvation.

May your wisdom always outsmart your thoughts.

Enjoy reading.

Ivonne

roles

partner, child, parent, entrepreneur
playing roles
following the accompanying rules
takes too much strength, energy
remembering lies and assumptions
always alert

decision
in all roles
be yourself
sometimes uncomfortable
but honest
how can it be easier?

noise, hassle, effort
stop
return
to your inner knowing
ask the question:
how can it be easy?

return
to your soul.
there you find clarity
vision, joy
this is your source
your roots

water your roots
move from your knowing
you can always
find the right tools
the right solutions
come to you

look back
you know
always
the answer
at the right moment
right?

you participate
be willing
grow
embrace uncomfortable moments
find growth

there is always more
that's how nature works
we are spiritual beings
having a human experience

your consciousness wants to grow

look at everything
the good
the bad
the ugly
follow your desire
100% your responsibility

I am the thinker

oh, I think this
only I think this
I see that I think

my thoughts
my story
is this true or...

everyone does this
everyone thinks
individually

I think this way
you think that way
and we think differently

that's how
we are made
as humans

realizing that
I think this
I only think in me

your own perception
blame & shame
is too easy

everything is energy

everything is energy
often said
but not always understood

everything is energy
not just
when it fits

methods are promoted
as the way
to make dreams come true

words give insight
when restless
you search

approach everything energetically
work from feeling
intuition
really?

focus on attention
observe energy
aware outside and inside
you are here

energy in your head
thoughts seek
how it works
what you experience

experience without analyzing
the situation IS
thoughts come and go
you just ARE

energy IS
no right or wrong
just the circumstance
try it, it's free

do you choose
struggle
or
acceptance?

we reason
investigate
the struggle with
WHAT IF

can you accept
that things
go
as they go?

get up from your meditation cushion
show up as who you are
do what comes up
or argue with it

bullshitradar

no commitment
will never change
energy and
situation

from a young age
seeking reassurance
with a bottle, a thumb, a cuddly toy
now peace in your head
feeling calmer

choice in thoughts
with a problem
get rid of it quickly
it eats away at you
restlessness runs your body

you do this to yourself
you don't allow yourself
you choose the victim role
no one can
influence your feeling

when changing
you have to give up something
habits of energy
money
time

invest in yourself
allow yourself
change
you are
worth it

you are more
than your obstacles
your happiness
is
one thought away

your built-in bullshit radar
tells you when
you're on the right path

but...
how often
do you listen to it?

upbringing, school, and society
encourage the opposite
prioritize reasoning and visible facts

performing life
trying to meet
someone else's standards

people get stuck
work no longer fits
burnout looming

live as you want
think as you want
experience what you want to experience

dive into your subconscious
discover limiting thoughts

do you trust your bullshit radar?

stop it

shit, I don't know what to do

how often do you hear that
or:
I find that difficult

I struggle with that
I always struggle, strange, right?
I don't know which way to go

you can say it once
but often, very often
at every encounter again....

the repetitive behavior
a feast for the subconscious
in the same bubble, on repeat

I'm not holier than you
I've done it myself
maybe still do

awareness of what you think and say
is the beginning
the cause

what you express
shows your worldview
what you believe

your happiness is one thought away

think stop it!

on repeat

how often do you run into a street lamp
how often do you run into a concrete wall
once already hurts, your body tells you

you treat physical pain immediately
why do we keep hurting
ourselves psychologically

we dwell on past scars
afraid of the future
worry, doubt, fear

the brain works like a computer
what you put in
you get out

just like a computer
needs updates
so do we

by constantly returning to old pain
you relive it and
stay stuck in a pattern

this is not denial of the past
but by feeling here and now
the pain can flow away

thoughts are energy
energy follows always
your attention

how often do you update
your inner computer
do you review your thoughts

you don't run into a wall 25 times either
eventually
you'll have a broken body

just being

humans are ingenious
the heart beats
breathing happens naturally
blood flows through the body

and yet....
we run away
with thoughts
that are just there too

we don't need to do anything with them
they're just there
we can choose
which ones to give attention to

what do you choose then?

simple but difficult

you have the words
in your head
you understand everything intellectually

and yet
the result is absent
how come?

the ego runs at full speed
wants to understand
seeks confirmation

your bullshit radar is on
you know something's right - or not
and yet you can't do it

you know the words
you know what to do
you're stuck in the vicious circle

old thoughts
old habits
your own internal formulas

the inner world remains invisible
how can you
keep trusting it

let go of how it always goes
how you always think
how you always do

total surrender to life
the vitality that flows through you
and is always there

in you, in me
your business, my business
because everything is energy

can it be so simple?
may it be so simple?
yes because it is so simple!

spiritual money

spirituality, awareness
energy work, and business
in my soul incompatible
making money with these elements
doesn't fit, isn't right, doesn't feel good

unbelievable beliefs
invisible walls in my mind
hinder the value I offer
honestly, I believed them too
these inventions of my subconscious

until I discovered
these thoughts
are just products
of my thinking
are they true?

what a power
to use
if I can
anyone can
because that's how we are made

being consistent
the urgency is
the inner calling
every day true to myself
no attacks,
no assumptions
doing my best

build a track record
start
continue
step outside the comfort zone
think beyond the limits
revise money mindset
enjoy

relationships are key
your relationshipcapital
clients are always there
selling without a relationship doesn't work
as a people pleaser, a challenge
try and fail
that's learning

connect

in the morning
before I open my eyes
I find myself in a space
where my thoughts
are not yet aware
of the stream of thoughts
rushing through my head.

one hand on my heart
the other on my belly
and I say:
every day comes as it comes

how nice
to feel this body again
what a wonder
what appears on my path

this morning
the coaching
the business reading
how special is that

I'm happy with this body
I love this body
even the parts
I'm sometimes less happy with

my belly
where I carried two children
nurtured them
and passed them on to the world

my fingers, which without thinking
prepare vegetables
type content
pick up a cup of coffee

my feet
carry me every day
my joints, that move by themselves
my heart, that pumps blood through my body

my senses
the gate to the outside
let life in
even when it's bullshit

my mind
my thinking
that works for or against me
as I choose to see it

thank you, body
for being there
so I can do
what I'm here to do

how simple

the simpler
the easier
the more effortless
it is to hear
the truth in you

if you worry
experience a lot of stress
worry about the how
annoyed that it's so slow
always looking back
it's already there

are you busy
or relaxed
are you in worry mode
or do you say stop
do you doubt and worry
or keep seeing opportunities

you can choose
what you want
what suits you
is worrying, doubt, and anxiety
a fixed part of you
why do you want that

your energy
your thoughts
your words
your pent-up anger
your restlessness
your doubt

your energy is your business

it happens in you

you can say stop
ask the question: is it true?
what if the thought isn't true?
what does this bring?
what possibilities then arise?

If you want a healthy energy balance, it's KEY to pause and notice what's happening within you—in your thoughts and your body.

This is what I enjoy the most: identifying where the subconscious gets stuck and contradicts itself.

By asking questions about what is truly True, based on what applies to everyone, you continu your discovery of who YOU are and what you're here to do.

criticism

have you ever felt
how criticism
lingers
and hurts?

words hit
as if you've been stabbed
words carry energy
vibration, power

words nourish
or destroy us
they transform what we say
and what we think.

our life is the result
of our thoughts
how do you let your thoughts
shape you?

start with healthy thoughts
nourish your brain
filter your words
avoid negativity, cherish love

invoke appreciation
even when you want to complain
positive communication
requires practice

it pays off

be grateful
express it
always create
a win-win

positive thoughts
bring strength
freedom
trust

the land beyond I don't know

the land beyond I don't know
is uncharted territory
where there is no clarity yet
where the world and the obvious end

the area where almost no one goes
because they don't know it exists
there are no signposts
just a desire to avoid fuss

a place to explore
with or without a map
with or without a guide
a deep dive into yourself

what do you have to lose?
what are you afraid of?
who will care?
what certainties can you leave behind?

the land beyond I don't know
a magical land
where you are the ruler
and the pawn

ease and peace are not static
they always move with you
so
even in the land beyond I don't know

ludo

if you don't roll the dice
you'll never get into the game

you won't move forward
you can't knock someone off the board

if you stay on the sidelines commenting
you'll never know which color suits you

you'll never win the game
it's about playing the game

you can't know in advance
what you'll roll with a dice
there's no technique
to roll a six

it's all about
picking up
the dice
start playing

you're in the game
sometimes you get frustrated
sometimes you don't.

playing the game
is
like entrepreneurship

words

words are just a fraction
of what we truly share
tone, heavily laden with meaning
body, a silent storyteller

how we speak
is more
than what we say

communication seems simple
between sender and receiver
boundaries blur
noise lurks
defenses rise

the subconscious
always listens
to tone, to body
unnoticed, yet powerful
it shapes thoughts and feelings

a harsh tone
a closed body
makes discomfort grow
withdrawel
even with gentle words

the subconscious filters
in the background
determines what we hear
it's not just about words
but how we carry them

explore your deepest layers
know that others think differently
check, observe
assume nothing, listen carefully
receive feedback in silence

uncertainty creates distance
awareness clears the way
for lighter communication
simplicity in conversation
lighter life

reset button

searching for peace
emptiness
filled with nothing
space

where is the reset button?
everything back to calm
how it used to be
simple

virus found
faced
felt
experienced

calm
thoughts come
and go
in and out

peace
emptiness
filled with nothing
space

reading glasses for thoughts

very sneaky
in the background
demanding
steering

straight into
the familiar
and trusted
mind trap

patterns
habits
reactions
as always

wanting to be right
attacking
convincing
pushing

blaming
expectations
disappointments
the same old story

unconsciously unhappy
not seeing it
searching for
your reading glasses for thoughts

hacked

everything goes wrong
no contact
see nothing
hear nothing

plug is out
no energy

can't do anything with it
program crashed
no hold
where is the hack?

turn around
see the connection
hear the words
feel the energy

connection with who you are
becomes leading
without all
the made-up stories

struggles

the inner conflict
not talking about money
yet wanting to earn it
unwilling to face the money story
yet wanting to receive money effortlessly

money is avoided
pricing is difficult
self-worth is a struggle
selling is yuck
sales pitches cause anxiety

what are you afraid of?
what could happen?
acting on beliefs
about money
is rooted in fear

everything is energy
you are energy
your beliefs are energy
your business is energy
money is energy

It's trendy these days to ask for high prices, and the high-end market is booming. However, only a few dare to look beneath the surface of the iceberg—both sellers and clients.
The internal struggle is often unfathomable, and no matter how beautifully it's presented, the solution isn't found there.

It takes discipline, perseverance, and courage to put on a snorkel and explore your subconscious, uncovering the hidden mountains of resistance.

Do you recognize this inner conflict?

formula

the business coach
has a formula
has a strategy
has a module

this works if you
fit the mold
adapt easily
resemble the coach

this doesn't work if
you don't know who you are
don't know what you want
don't know why it's not working

you are unique
your business is unique
your strategy is unique
you are not a copy

learn to listen
to who you are
to what you want
discover your internal vision

surrender
you don't need to fight anymore
step into trust
everything is already there!

dare

daring to surrender
to who you are
what you want
chaos and turmoil arise

not logical
always
everything
safe and secure

allow yourself
you can learn this
you already have it
you already are it

the only thing you need to do
is allow yourself
to receive
who you are

this sounds simple
and it is
your thinking
makes it difficult!

true colours

coming out
facing it
saying it
who I am

super scary
omg what will "they" think
for years
I didn't follow my desires

"they" have all sorts of opinions
I stand my ground
despite the heaviness
I went along for too long

it's time now
the desire
burns inside
I am ready

I take steps
I take action
I am visible
waaahhaa

inhale and exhale
whew, I'm still here
it wasn't that bad
so, what do I want now?

We make the process of change and following our desires seem so huge in our minds that it literally becomes its own chapter. When you're stuck in your head, you're disconnected from yourself and your desires.

Standing up for YOURSELF is like coming out. Of course, it's scary—the old beliefs scream in your mind that it's unsafe to step out of what's familiar.

What can you expect?? You don't know, and because we've learned that we must know everything in advance, we avoid taking new steps. Such a waste—through experience, I know the more uncomfortable you feel, the closer you are to your desire. The law of polarity is at work here.

Do you show your true self to yourself, your environment, and your clients?

inner house

inhabit your inner house
as you inhabit
your physical house
taking care
nurture

is your house insulated
double glazing
good cavity walls
draft-free floors
roof with wool insulation
crawl space filled with pearls
so the energy stays inside

and the inner house
how do you sit in this perfectly insulated house?
how do you keep your energy inside?
nurture the energy of your inner house?
is this inner house insulated?
do you live only under the roof?
are all doors and windows open?
or do you decide when they open?

do you inhabit all parts of your inner house?
do you take good care of all the rooms?
where do you leak your energy?
fears, scarcity thinking?
dependence on others?
not daring?
doubt?

Your energy is your business

Your energy is the foundation of your business. If you give it away easily and unconsciously, it directly impacts your business.

Dare to be brutally honest with yourself and identify where you leak energy. Take the time to explore all parts of your inner house and truly experience them.

The hardest parts, the ones we avoid because they are too painful, are often hidden behind lock and key. Or so you think. Your subconscious believes this, but it's a lie—these feelings linger in the background, along with the stories attached to them.

All feelings, all parts of you, make you who you are NOW.

gift

unwrapping your unique gift
everything in nature comes with a mission
it's here for a reason

the oak is already programmed in the acorn
the sheep in the lamb
the sunflower in the seed

everything in nature has a purpose
is meaningful
is part of the whole

humans are part of nature
each with a special purpose
well packaged within us

sometimes a hard package
sometimes a soft package
sometimes transparent cellophane
sometimes opaque glass

carefully
tear it open
damages
pick at it
oops, watch out

let someone else do it
this is painful
not this shit
no, better do it yourself
take personal responsibility

it's up to us to unwrap this gift ourselves
to undergo life's tests
people on your path
challenging situations
shitty moments

varied emotions
sadness
anger
joy
love

and the unwrapping itself
continues and each time
there are tests and hints
and it's up to us to recognize them
to hear, feel, and see them

you think, "now I'm there"
then a new hint comes
layer by layer you unwrap your gift
sometimes with tears
sometimes smoothly

and then suddenly it becomes lighter
a glimmer
an energy boost
a quantum leap
enlightenment

a deeper layer
you feel increasingly lighter
thoughts have less influence
you experience space
and you do what you are here to do!

all equal

I am exactly the same
made just like you
I breathe
you breathe

what and how
I don't know
joint adventure
breath and energy

I have thoughts about you
you have thoughts about me
pleasant, good, kind
fearful, angry, jealous

all with their own frequency
searching for that one pleasant feeling
the feeling of being supported
being one

thoughts are still formless
until actions give them form
a service, product, or even a business
a dream becomes reality

you perceive this
you become aware
you see it
you sense it

vegetable garden

A vegetable garden is just like entrepreneurship. I always enjoy finding the connections in life.

This year, I started a vegetable garden with friends. Although my parents always had one when I was younger, I wasn't really aware of it back then.

As a teenager, I found it incredibly annoying to help with weeding from time to time.

Here's how I see the link with entrepreneurship:

First
inquiring
investing
unaware
filled with desire
exited
what will come out of it

you start sowing
good seed in potting soil
watering
not too much, or they'll drown
and then, yes
the first sprouts find their way to the surface
what a joy

then the next phase
repotting to a larger pot
a slightly more mature pot
good soil in it
still incredibly vulnerable
still need to watch the nutrients
and just let them grow

oh dear
attackers from the outside appear
this year, it was slugs
in large numbers
crisis
what now?
eggshells, escar go

the first lettuce
the first zucchini
the first tomatoes
the first arugula
the first peppers
the first herbs
wow, the harvesting can begin

sanctuary

your sanctuary
can sound heavy
can sound delightful
can sound airy
can sound expansive

your sanctuary is who you are
how you think
how you feel
how you behave
everything originates from your sanctuary

do you let someone in uninvited?
do you let feelings in uninvited,
such as hate, envy, irritation, distrust?

your sanctuary
is your place
here, your rules apply
what you stand for
you are the boss

in your sanctuary
you tolerate no excuses
you are honest with yourself
you are gentle with yourself
you are always there

your sacred safe place
where a fountain of love flows
continuously
where you can bathe in love
where you find warmth

the place where your divinity resides
where you meet God
from this sanctuary, you may take steps
from this sanctuary, from this fine energy
from this love, you may be yourself

from this safety
you can face uncertainty
you can step outside

from this love
you can be seen
from the warmth you feel
you can face the cold outside
connect with another

your sanctuary is in you
is always with you
it's not about you
it's not not about you
you just need to be

From this safe place, you can handle anything, make bold moves both personally and professionally, and choose what YOU truly want.

Do you feel there's more to life for you? Do your inner insecurities and dependencies hold you back?

Your energy is your business; without attention, there is no growth.

Can you see where your subconscious holds you back? Are you doing what you need to do and making money from what you're really good at?

I didn't understand you before

I didn't understand what my feeling was
I was happy, sad
angry, joyful
scared, brave

with a therapist
it didn't feel right
I said nothing
something must be wrong with me

I didn't feel it right
the "pro" knows what they're doing
I can't feel
I don't know

and so on
and so on
and so on
until

shit
I've always had it right
I didn't listen to you
I didn't understand you

I've experienced this many times in my quest to discover who I am and what I'm here to do. With several therapists, coaches, healers, and readers— you name it—I could tell they were projecting their own issues. I said nothing because I saw myself as less than them.

The penny dropped after a program with an American coach, and then her coach, and then a few more. Clearing your own issues before helping someone with energetic work is incredibly important. If you do this work, you know that Everything Is Energy, but do you truly understand it?

I see and speak with many energy workers who fall short in this area, who don't have a coach to support them, and believe that everything can be resolved on an energetic or emotional level.
Unfortunately, that's not the case. As humans, we carry our conditioning with us, which comes with all sorts of opinions on personal growth and often prefers safe and certain choices.

freedom

seeing is not believing
believing is seeing

the senses aren't
what's true
who you are is
what's true

conditioning
versus
truth

dependency
versus
independence

stuck
versus
light

prison
versus
freedom

Last week, I enjoyed a Christmas movie where Santa Claus said the wise words, "Seeing is not believing, believing is seeing."

This made me reflect, and I realized this statement applies not only to Christmas movies but also serves as a powerful metaphor for life and entrepreneurship.

As an entrepreneur, you might be inclined to want to know the outcome first and cling to it. While this may work temporarily, you'll eventually get stuck in uncertainty because you can't fully control the results. You end up in a dead end.

Letting go of the need to control the outcome and instead believing in who you are and what you're here to do leads to greater success. It's about staying true to yourself and the essence of who you are.

Though it may be difficult for your mind to let go of control, this process is about surrender. Belief in yourself and the path you're meant to walk opens the door to more possibilities and long-term success.

elusive

it's elusive
you just can't get
where you want to go
the level of joy
and satisfaction falls
below sealevel

the invisible
resistance
leads you through a maze
of questions
doubts
worries

how come?

you set your goal
you want to do it, and yet
damn
not again
not yet
when then?

you feel stupid
too dumb
you are disappointed

what if you stop believing this story?

I was trapped in this rollercoaster, too. You don't understand it; you keep thinking and overthinking where the solution might be hidden.

But it's simpler and easier than you can imagine: What's the cause of the effect? It's how you think and what you allow.
I also cursed my coaches for talking about it so easily when it felt like such a tough battle not to be yourself.

Unveiling the invisible blocks in the subconscious of entrepreneurs is what I enjoy most. It's a magical moment when the light goes on in their eyes.
It's remarkable how you can move through confusion and create space for growth and success, both personally and professionally.

ego drug

fishing for approval
confirmation, making an impression
costs you energy

and is not a good investment
of your energy
you drain yourself

it's a short-term ego drug
and without insight
you fall into the trap

every day again
this circus—"how do i get more"
in my pre-programmed way?

being in service
is truly
helping yourself

effectively managing
your time
the time of another

you gain energy
the roi
is astounding

Being in service is key to your development in your role within a business or organization.

Continuously ask yourself: How can I make more room for the love, divinity, and energy that flows through me, and use it to help others move forward?

psycho-logical

in trust
in surrender
dare to surrender
let go
only then can you succeed

yes, that's easy to say
but what about
the voices in your head
the fears
the doubts

my experience is
that with trembling knees
and sweaty armpits
I found it incredibly nerve-wracking
to let go of control.

to say no to
the familiar voices in my head
to say no to
the story I believed about myself
to say that this was a lie

frustration and irritation
remain bewildered
as do disappointment
bitterness
and loneliness

you don't do this just like that
you don't really believe it at first
your doubts are served up to you
the more psycho-logical your thoughts are
the better the outcomes

part of

the rose doesn't think
which petal to open first
left or right

the caterpillar doesn't worry
about how on earth
to wriggle out the butterfly
an inside job

the oak doesn't ask
the beech whether
to grow acorns
from beech nuts

the sun doesn't
take thursdays off
because it doesn't feel like
shining

gravity
remains in force
despite the bad weather
despite money or time issues

the sea doesn't stop
with ebb and flow
the positive always stands
opposite the negative.

everything comes
everything goes
all in its own time

When you read this, you probably think, "Of course, that sounds logical." You think this because you are unconsciously competent in the universal laws.

Everything in nature, including us humans, operates based on the same universal laws: the rose that blooms, the caterpillar that transforms, the oak that grows, the sun that rises, and gravity that keeps us grounded.

We've been taught that we should be able to solve all problems intellectually, that we need to understand everything, preferably with a quick fix.

But what if there's another, more psycho-logical way?

A way that trusts you're part of a whole, without drifting off into the clouds, and that, if you understand how you're made, you can maintain more peace and focus.

but how do I get there?

nice words
intuition, inner voice
inside, from within
also for me

what is intuition
how do I actually know
when is it that one voice
the voice of my true self

where are you
my deeper self
the soft sound
the whisper of words

if I hear you
I can follow you
if I hear you
it will be okay

everyone says so
listen from within
then it will be fine
then everything is solved

where are you
I want to hear you
I want to get to know you
I'm done with the other voices in my head

I'm always here
you just don't hear me
you're just listening to another channel
I'm here, now it's up to you

I'm the voice
the feeling that strives for growth
you often don't want to hear it
you'd rather not listen to it

if then?

if I take a course
if I have everything ready
if I have more time
if the kids are back at school
if I have the money

if I quit my job
if I have more space for myself
if I finish my program
if I have a client
if my mission is clear

if I have worked out my vision
if my funnel is ready
if I have discussed it with my partner
if I lose x kilos
if I have a ton in the bank

if I have a babysitter
if I meditate more
if I have space to...
if I'm done with my excuses
if I no longer tolerate this

then, yes, then I can really start

Pffft.

We come up with so many excuses to avoid starting what we truly want! Yes, I've been there, done that—until I got so fed up that I stopped delaying and overthinking.

Thankfully, that time is far behind me.

I remember how much money, energy, and time it cost, all of which could have been better invested in moving forward rather than stubbornly clinging to old beliefs. When you dare to examine what's really underneath with a fresh and clear perspective, you can step over the threshold of your own stagnant beliefs.

labels

so many people
so many desires
words
to understand things
is that really so?

or is it a way to get further
from what it's really about?
sometimes I wonder
or is it just our program
that wants this

I look at the energy
and then information comes
just from the energy
from the frequency of the name
an error for the thoughts

another name
it's about the same

all about energy
about infinite intelligence
god
whatever label we put on it

through reading
remote viewing, shamanism, healing
coaching, training, quantum jumping
clearings, crystals

reiki, dowsing rods, oils, biotensors
massages, words, writing
drawing, painting, sculpting, modeling
and you label it

one method is no better
or worse than another
that's the programming
some call it the ego

no competition and rivalry
just creativity and competence
in experiencing
just energy

ways, methods
techniques
to connect
to move energy

differences are logical
we are all human
we are made
in the same way

only
programmed differently and
activated in diverse ways

your trigger
enters your thoughts
positively or negatively

your energy moves

energy is neutral
it doesn't matter
the label we assign

I see you

I am invisible
I listen to
the voices of
what has been proven
this is how it's done

do it this way
then you get more

if you do this
then ………
follow me
then …….
discover
then …….
develop
then …….

but who am I
then …..

why do I have to do
what works for you
listening to your
inner voice
what it tells you

why can't I
discover who I am
listen to
my inner voice

discover what is
inside me
discover and
then……

discover
which movement
is inside me
experience

why so many words
how come
I am here
I don't want to
search anymore

I am ready
I surrender
I am trust
I am the movement
I am the energy

I am what I emit
I follow my frequency
I listen within

I hear the movement
I feel the movement
I direct the movement

others see me
oh dear
I am visible
to myself

and visible
to others

faking or shaking

fake it till you make it
I don't want that
I don't want to fake
I want to shake

why do I have to
wear a certain jacket
why do I have to
look this way

why so
why
don't I have confidence
in the way I am being

why don't I believe
in my own message
why don't I acknowledge
what I'm good at

why do I believe that
why do I deny myself play
why do I deny myself pleasure
why do I deny myself just being

why do I deny myself
just experiencing
experiencing what is
allowing how I want to respond

which movement
comes from me
the natural movement
that only I can be

that I believe in me
in my message
and not in someone else's

my message
my energy
this is how
I'm shaking

truth

listen to what's underneath
don't accept
what is said
words that cover up
what lies beneath

listen to what lies beneath
the fear
the insecurity
the sadness
that which is hidden

sometimes without realizing it
sometimes consciously
but too painful
to look at
no room yet

what can't
be seen and experienced
what is unsafe
unfamiliar
uncomfortable

by experiencing
by truly answering
brutally honestly
answering what
lives inside you

that it is there
brings light
brings relief
clarity
space

listen deeper
don't assume
trust your antenna
the antenna that resonates and connects
with the antenna of the other

connection from
the depth
the love
the infinite
the energy

I think this
in my thinking
you think that
we label
everything

label here
label there
label everywhere

who are you really
what do you show
what do we really know about each other

label from me or you
that is what I
no longer trust

look behind the story
listen really
hear what is not said

trust
your inner voice
your truth

peace

no fuss
no chatter
no blah blah
no unrest

the peace
as a foundation
to
be

I tolerate
this peace
the other
no longer

I allow
I surrender
I am the peace
the foundation

this foundation
to
build
peace

lost

lost
in the alleys
of my thinking
lost in space

away from the feeling
wandering
searching
where am I

I doubt
I work a lot
I give a lot
I compensate

I am exhausted
no energy
I leak energy
I don't know how

can you help
which way
should I go
what is my path

what is good
for me
and the other
the connection

on repeat

it's easy especially for you
why make such a problem of it
why

you can just do that
why do you find that difficult
why

why are you afraid of it
why can't you do it
why

yeah just do it
pffft
and that's it

you feel it beforehand
and shy away
you don't do it

people
around you
see you as you are

see your abilities
what you do
what you can

don't understand
why you don't
take the right actions

they see your outside
this differs from
your inside

you don't yet know how good you are
you don't yet know how you come across
you don't yet know who you are
you don't yet know that story about yourself

the old story of
I don't know
I can't
I don't know what I want
is still on your auto-repeat

wakey wakey

We try so hard not to be ourselves that the process becomes difficult and challenging.

This requires brutal honesty with yourself and making space for the world that exists within you.

now what?

okay clear
but later
now everything
is clear
I know what I have to do

after 1 hour
1 day
1 week
I don't know anymore
then what?

what should I do?

choose another thought
that sounds too easy
too simple
saying that I
think in lies too

whether I tried it?
whether I really live my insights?
whether I say that the thought is a lie?
whether I limit my self-sabotage?
eh no not that

oh yes I see it now, logical
that everything will stay the same
I need to address how I think

I allow myself to say no
to my thinking
I can be brutally honest

because I am already enough, worthy, and lovable!

The question often arises: HOW can I live this in daily life?
Simply by no longer believing the thoughts that ask, " how?" If you don't truly apply the insights, nothing changes. There is no magic formula or pill you can buy; this is your own journey here on earth, and you can choose how to experience it!

I am here

I am always with you
it is completely okay
you know
I hear you
I see you
I feel you
I experience what you experience

that is all
I see you
it is all well
you are always exactly where you need to be
even if you don't feel it
for a moment
you can always lean on me

are you lost in
in the darkest corners of your thoughts
where you think you are alone
I am with you there too
only you can't see me anymore
you can't feel me anymore
but I am right beside you

I am loyal to you
you are always right
when you speak from your truth
your truth from the highest version of you
is good for you
is good for the other
I trust you

I am always here for you
you can experience
thanks to you I can see
thanks to you I can hear
thanks to you I can speak
thanks to you I can smell
thanks to you I can experience

You are here on this planet to experience life, and the coolest part is that, as a free spirit, you can choose how you want to experience it.

When things are tough, it's hard to see the blue sky through the clouds. Even though you know it's there, it remains difficult to surrender to that truth.

When you feel frustrated, lost, or restless, return to the silence within yourself. Yes, it may sound cliché, and as if it's all so simple.

Well, it is simple—if you surrender, truly surrender, to what is.

What thought can bring peace to your mind right now?

I am experiencing

I experience through you
I see through your eyes
I hear through your ears
I smell your surroundings
I speak through your mouth
I think through your thoughts
I feel the touch through your touch
I feel the touch of someone else
I can distinguish
I can experience

thank you
this is the greatest gift you give me
thanks to you I can live
don't lock yourself in a prison
because then I can't live
you can't live either
and that is a shame
because we are made for each other
you are the body
and I am the spirit

together we are one
and we have to do this together
so let's please become friends
jump over hurdles together
I will support you with every hurdle there is
let's go together
let's fly together
let's experience together
let's experience together
to see, to hear, to speak, and to play

shall we really start living now?

You are not alone. Even when you don't know where to turn, you are never truly alone. You always have your Self with you—you can't escape it. If you feel bad, who is experiencing that feeling? If you worry, who is doing the worrying? We lose a lot of our energy to negative emotions, and it's a waste of your precious energy.

weeds

my thinking
is mine
I remove the weeds
I listen
speak to myself

thoughts root like weeds
focus on what can go wrong or
what holds you back
let these thoughts grow
your head gets full

I don't want that
I keep my thinking
colorful and calm
because
"I can trust my Self!"

there comes
light
peace
space
trust

heaviness

I choose heaviness
I prefer that
always done
don't like it
but yeah habit

a kind of martyrdom
don't do it consciously
not on purpose
I'm annoyed by it too
but yeah habit

know
if you say this
then you are aware
that you do this
how can you still say it then

don't repeat it
don't say it more than once
abstain from
compulsive
addicted heaviness

law of polarity
everything has two sides
opposite of heaviness
is light
you can choose light

You can only choose NOW how you want to experience your life. The stories running through your mind relate to old junk that probably isn't even yours.

I know it but...

I get distracted
a lot is asked of me
I have to
the "I know it but" story

(underneath plays)
what if I say no
what if they don't like me anymore
what if I am successful
what if I have no time

(underneath it)
what if I fail
what if I am not good enough
what if I don't deserve this

(underneath it)
am I lovable

turn it around

I am lovable
I am worthy
I am good enough
I can handle everything

it is always the right time
I am successful
I am valuable
I am independent
I set my boundaries
for others
and especially for myself
for my thoughts

I live
that is Truth

I want it
I go for it
I pay the price
I give this to myself
this change in me

I put in the hours
this change demands
I step into my recalibrated self

I no longer tolerate my behavior
that drags me down
that makes me stop

I say goodbye to my old habits
I say goodbye to my old beliefs
I say goodbye to the story of myself
the story I believed

changing
setting boundaries for others
setting boundaries for myself
is hard

I don't believe it anymore
it had cost too much
it is a lie
that I believed since my birth

I am already a success
I got up this morning
and I'm still here
that is the truth

If you truly want things to be different, you'll do everything to make it happen. Then, you'll recognize that whatever comes up is either an opportunity or a learning moment. You'll also need to say goodbye to the way things have always been, and sometimes that includes people who can't see or accept your change. When you're true to yourself and let this trust grow within you, you gradually turn up the light inside until you're fully in it.

We are so conditioned not to listen to our own will, which makes it difficult for many to allow themselves the space to embrace this.

Are you doing what you truly want?

holding back

holding yourself back
not expressing
what you're good at
out of fear
for the judgment
of the other
of yourself
are you self-absorbed

what's the point
of keeping yourself small
not being visible
wanting to conform to
how things have always been
how people know you
adjusting and adjusting

know that you are then manipulating
adjusting is manipulating your behavior
you mix your unique self
with the energy of others

what if it's not about you
you are an instrument
you have a gift
that only you can offer

that only through you must enter the world
it's not about your identity
not about your story
who you think you should be

show yourself and be heard
you are worth it
your clients are worth it
it is your duty

show yourself
your unique gift
who are you
who you are meant to be

yes but

how often do you say this

that's true, but...
yes, I hear what you're saying, but...
I know, but...
of course, but...
you're absolutely right, but...
I'm going to do it, but...

if you start paying attention
how often we say this

we stay stuck in our own story
and yes, me too
I'm no holier than thou

the story you keep telling yourself
and keep coming back to
where you seek confirmation
from yourself
from others
online or offline

pfft exhausting

while it's just a story
a composition of your thoughts

what if you choose
different thoughts
thoughts that
create a different story

and therefore
different reactions!

no more fighting

you don't need to fight anymore
surrender, just stop
the battle is over
let life
take its course

you can't control this
you can't steer it
you can only surrender
detach from how it should be
let go of how you think it should be

this isn't giving up
it's not throwing in the towel
it's allowing yourself
it's making space
for the peace that you are

it's not about you
and it's also not not about you
you are responsible
for the choices you make
in your thoughts and actions

so from inside and outside!

being brutally honest in your internal process
without drowning in it
blaming others
using it as an excuse
for where you are in life now

being brutally honest
requires
discipline and courage

see your truth within yourself
stop canceling yourself!

thinking not right

your way of thinking is not right
excuse me
you're not thinking correctly
an attack
immediate defense
I'm right, you're not

busy proving
to myself and others
voicing accusations
shame lurks
all hands on deck
we're sinking

only because someone came
who said I wasn't thinking right
pissed
why?
who is this person
my coach

consistent in generating revenue
peace of mind
takes responsibility
I couldn't see it
I cursed the coach
I knew it was the Ttruth

my business wasn't working
my way of thinking
confusion
I didn't understand it
alienated
out of connection

ego says
I'm not dumb
I pick things up quickly
I know how energy works
yet something slipped by me, but what?
my thinking? no, that couldn't be it!

keeping up appearances outwardly
while it eats you up inside
said to myself:
"how dumb of me not to see this"
to my clients, I said:
"experience first, feel after."

subconscious make-belief
I thought I was doing well
but I analyzed, considered
postponed
until it was never good enough

my thinking
about myself wasn't right

let go of control
let go of structure
let go of habits
let go of lifebuoys
the Truth lies deeper

where in your life
is it going differently than desired?
examine your thoughts,
write them down
read them back
ask yourself if these beliefs

align with universal truth
because that says:
you are already a success

name

your name
your energy
the energy of your origin

my name
my energy
the energy of my origin

when marrying
when adopted
when not wanting to be found

your name
when marrying
I carry your name

and the energy
of your name
of your origin

it feels safe
familiar
like it's always been

it's easy
one name
for the outside world

where is my name
my energy
the energy of my origin

confusion
who am I really
this feels like a lot

even if it feels good
the relationship is good
there's something

so much to carry
energies that
you can't do anything with

where expectations
are locked up
and so are you

choose your energy
choose how you want to feel
choosing is your responsibility

A name has a frequency, and this frequency is composed of information from your family, previous generations, past lives, etc.

We don't often think about how much energy is tied to a name. As soon as a woman takes her husband's name, or when you take or receive a different name (e.g., through adoption), you automatically take on the energy of that name.

The reason why you take the name also plays a role. Whether it was for protection, safety, habit, or was forced, your energy becomes subordinate to the energy of the name you take on.

This process is so subtle that it only reveals itself later in life when you want to stand up for yourself, hesitate to take action for your own growth, or remain invisible.

In a reading, these two different energies become clearly visible, and patterns and underlying processes are clarified. This helps you see where and how you can regain safety and confidence in yourself and your energy.

show up

showing up
in thoughts
in word
in action

easy
flawless
simple
no way

practice makes perfect
discipline
noticing it
faster each time

feeling the pull
of negativity
of dishonesty
this only happens within me

step out of this energy
return inward
to peace
to clarity

what was I believing
which thoughts
which feelings
which attack

what was I repeating
where did I want to be right
what didn't my ego want
and it clears up

the lightness
is back
the space
is back

it always starts with you
you are it
the center of the universe
this is a law of nature

letting go

letting go
sounds
so easy
often difficult

and yet
it's simple
energy goes where
the attention is

everything has an opposite
that is a law of nature
so difficult
becomes easy

if your business isn't going well
you're not going well
focus on what you want
dare to surrender

surrender to the unknown
gross, that's scary
and fun
and surprising

you don't know what will happen
the little voice wants to know everything in advance
to convince you not to do it
because it knows it's losing ground

you do it
you let the little voice
shout in your thoughts
and turn the volume down

surrendering to the unknown
we aren't taught this
we grow up with safety and security
where not knowing isn't safe
we are so ingeniously made
to trust
our internal compass

desire

how do I want it
oh dear I don't say how I want it

I always say
I'll do it
just let me
do you want that? okay, me too

and then...

suddenly you discover
do I still want this
I'm caught up in a play
and I'm playing a minor role

a clone of
how parents did it
how it's supposed to be
to fit in

I want this to be different
first forced
uncomfortable
it stands out

friction within
and outside
standing up for yourself
regardless of the reaction

and oops, I fall back in
I get stuck in it
don't want to disappoint
don't want to get hurt

get back up
I set boundaries
to all those thoughts
that bring me down

I believe in myself
I trust myself
I'm worth it

Changing and clearly setting your boundaries causes friction because you wonder: how will others handle this, how will they respond?

As a child, you were dependent on your parents and environment and did everything to fit in for safety and survival.

As an adult, situations still arise that ask you to look at areas where you are not yet emotionally mature, which is why they trigger you. It requires attention to explore these parts of yourself, as they are also part of you and want to be acknowledged.

The main reason we don't trust ourselves is because we were told that we didn't really feel what we felt, or that what we felt was unacceptable.

I want it now

I want it
I really want it
I'm going for it
I want it now

I'm in a flow
I'm in the feeling
people come to me
want to work with me

uh can I do this
can I ask this price
am I not too expensive
I block

ended back in my head
overthinking everything
they'll never pay me
how

but how?

the question "but how"
people seek speed
practical solutions
to turn thoughts into deeds
from within

we all know those phases
up and down ebb and flow
natural laws in our existence

when ebb lasts too long
it's time to find the cause
understand the effect

different versions of you already exist
in the layers of the universe
you are present now

if you start thinking about it
then comes the confusion
because how can this be realized?

If you start thinking about it, you get caught in a mind trap, and the next "but how" pops up.

Fortunately, physicists have pondered this and proven that everything is energy and that everything in the universe follows the same universal laws.

We often doubt ourselves because we were told our feelings were either invalid or wrong.

popular to live in your head

as a child you live freely
you do what feels right
fall get up keep going

you grow up learn to create programs
for others to be nice
you learn how things should be
you get stickers for good behavior
your head fills with rules

slowly your attention shifts
from body to head
you learn to think
plan choose goals
and get used to living in your head

the inner voice becomes quiet
with every new step
adjusting performing keeping others happy
you live in your head because it's safe
you feel no but say yes
your head screams your body whispers

until your body screams
it can no longer whisper
a burnout a halt

how did it get to the point
that the voice inside
fell silent
that we no longer know
how to hear ourselves?

Your body literally tells you to stop. It's unfortunate, but if you won't listen, you'll have to feel it.
How bizarre is it that we've turned down the wisdom of our body—the inner voice, our intuition—so low that we no longer hear it or even know how to tune into it?

almost

postponing
making a call
being visible
solving problems
making a decision
paying a bill
making an appointment
standing up for yourself

from the moment
you know it
the circus
of thoughts begins
focused on what you have to do

various scenarios
start to surface
good and bad
the action to be taken
waits patiently

and then after long deliberation
lots of thoughts
lots of thoughts
and even more thoughts
finally the action follows

your head clears up
the tangle of thoughts ends
the peace settles
this is what i want in the future

next time
I'll make the decision earlier
pay the bill immediately
call instead of email
keep control instead of my thoughts

I have experienced this decision-making process myself, and I also see it with my clients. Once the decision is made, peace arises. Do you recognize this too? Dreading something because of a mountain of thoughts, but once you've done it, it's over.

from within

knowing who you are
what triggers you
how it feels
what you want

the movement
that moves forward
the movement
that stagnates

setting boundaries for yourself
not getting lost in drama
acting from trust
daring to take action

being visible from your internal vision
knowing that the inner presence is always there
trusting in it
the body shows the way

surrendering to the moment
parking your thoughts for a while
trusting that everything is fine
believing that everything is fine

experiencing and learning
constantly expanding your awareness

it's simple
turn your thinking from a to z off
turn your body on
aligned thinking from a to b

being in the moment
experiencing what is
without the story
you believe coming in between

about who you thought you were
about who someone else is
who should be
who the other should be

so complicated
so stressful
so useless
so disconnected

you are not here
lost in
past and
future

in this moment
everything happens
only now
you are now

what would you like to experience
fuss or peace
fear or trust
you always choose!

Running your business and leading from your own internal vision brings a lot of peace and confidence.
Are you ready to overcome a few bumps and step into life with full commitment to yourself?

free from

free from
what
what do you mean
free from what

free from
how someone else reacts
what someone else says
who you have in front of you

what do you mean
i don't understand
free from how
who what

free from
the confirmation
the recognition
the need to be heard and seen

independent in
thinking
feeling
experiencing

no one can hurt you
you experience hurt
no one can ignore you
you experience being ignored

you are the center
of the universe
you
not someone else

this is free from
you choose
you experience
you are the core

realizing this
being aware
daring
is being free from

free from
what
what do you mean
free from what

free from
how someone else reacts
what someone else says
who you have in front of you

what do you mean
i don't understand
free from how
who what

free from
the confirmation
the recognition
the need to be heard and seen

independent in
thinking
feeling
experiencing

no one can hurt you
you experience hurt
no one can ignore you
you experience being ignored

you are the center
of the universe
you
not someone else

this is free from
you choose
you experience
you are the core

realizing this
being aware
daring
is being free from

When I first started with my spiritual coach in 2008, I was living in my head and didn't understand this concept. In my general consciousness, it felt very abstract and intangible. I had never experienced anything like this before and didn't know how it could be understood on deeper levels.

Since 2016, in addition to my spiritual coach, I've worked with other coaches and mentors to discover this within myself, which has allowed my awareness to keep expanding.

Your awareness grows every moment. For example, if you look up now and see a cloud that wasn't there before, that's an expansion of your awareness.

I'm becoming increasingly aware of these insights and experiences in life. Are you aware that you are experiencing life on a moment-to-moment basis?

what you say
is what you are

what you say to yourself
you find normal
seems like reality
but honestly
you would never say it to someone else

you're not aware
of the daily
automatic
chatter snarls and nitpicking
at yourself

take a look
step back
write it down
and discover
that it's garbage

a waste of your time
a waste of your self-worth
to still believe this stream of
thoughts
draw a line and say stop!

Setting boundaries for the stream of thoughts is something that often gets overlooked. We clearly set boundaries in the external world but forget to do so internally.

We often take our way of thinking for granted, saying, "that's just how I think," but this is precisely where boundaries are needed.

When your internal boundaries are clear, external boundaries become less necessary.

no clue

client:
"I have a big mission
I want to help x people with
this and that problem
I'm really good at it
achieve really great results"

me: what are you struggling with
"I have no clients
expressing what I actually do
I just can't do it
because it's a bit weird"

me: do you mean that what you do is weird
"no I absolutely know for sure
that I'm good and really make a difference
but I can't share this
because
……(and comes a variation of the following sentences)
· not sure yet (oops you just said you were)
· what words (oops you just said you were)
· how to say this simply (oops you just said it quite simply)"
and then:
"it's really a bit too bizarre for words that you know this from such a reading"

yup true every time, and you know what I marvel at it every time and you know why?

well

because I'm not concerned with the story I believe about myself, and how I can best come across, what I should say, why I should say it, and to whom

you have that choice too!

body to head and back

wow this feels good
my body
my energy
my being
all clear now

1 day later
so nice I'm going to get started
wow it feels good
I can take on the world
I'm really going to take steps now

I'm in my business now
so what should I do
how am I going to do it
the attention shifts
from body to head

hmm oh yeah that feeling
let me think
how did it feel again
okay but what am I going to do now
how am I going to do this

1 week later
what did I write down
again last week
hmm oh yeah that feeling
let me think

how did it feel again
okay but what am I going to do now
how am I going to do this
the attention shifts
from body to head

and so the circle keeps turning
continuously in your head
you really want to
you feel it now

only you don't know how

How can you integrate this energetic work? Often, you do energetic exercises or meditations, and it feels great because, in the energetic world, everything is always in harmony.

But as soon as you open your eyes, the visible world comes back into focus, feeding you information. Immediately, you fall back into your habits and patterns of dealing with things. This is where the challenge lies—becoming aware of these habits, highlighting them, and setting boundaries. This is often where the process gets stuck.

At this point, it becomes painfully clear that what you've always tried to hide is now visible. The very thing you avoid facing is often your next step forward.

If there's a lot of chaos and unrest, understand that your subconscious is rebel-

knowing who you are

who should i be
to make this my business
I believe I have to be someone
who does the same as everyone else
because that works
so it will work for me too

who should I be
I'll use exactly the same formula
I'll follow exactly the same strategy
as I'm told
because that's going to work
that's what I was promised

who should I be
who should I be
searching for the inside
is not to be found on the outside
you don't
have to be anyone at all

you already are
all the ingredients
are present
all the formulas
are present
you are already a success

You start one step behind if you don't listen to yourself. You've already lost everything because you've lost yourself in the process.

It's sad to see this happen to many small entrepreneurs—they stop believing in themselves. Once they get stuck in their heads and start believing the story they keep repeating, it becomes hard to stop the cycle.

Do you know who you are BEING?

frequency of words

words in content
words from you
borrowed words
frequently used words

borrowed words
don't carry your weight
don't reach the other
are like a dime a dozen

your own words
reach a deeper layer
the energy is palpable
even between the letters

your authority
your authenticity
from your originality
you who are

Words are magical tools that bring your message to life through speech or writing. How original you are comes from your words, from the way you express the feelings inside you.

From my own experience and that of my clients, I know this can be quite challenging, especially because we are constantly bombarded with information on social media and television. Our brains are so brilliant at absorbing all this information, which makes it difficult to find our own words amidst the chaos.

I often hear from clients that, after listening to the business reading a few times, I was able to put words to the feelings they had inside.

How is that possible? Let me explain: When you have a radio, you can search for various frequencies to listen to different stations. You can't see the radio waves, but you know they are there, and you can find them with the radio.

That's what happens in a reading. I am the radio, and I search for the frequency that belongs to your company's name and your name. Then, the words come.

one thought away

your happiness is one thought away
this sentence is from sydney banks
beautiful
the simplicity so graceful

what a drama we make of it ourselves
we give the thoughts of drama
a huge stage
and perform it day after day

such a shame isn't it
even if you've always done it that way
why continue if it
doesn't work

don't entertain that thought
don't make a soap opera out of it
step out of the drama
choose another thought

back to simplicity
recognize when you think yourself stuck
acknowledge that you're doing it
then you can choose another thought

simple
easy
just Being

These internal soap operas cause us to unconsciously build up energetic blockages. We don't understand why things aren't working and start looking for answers outside ourselves.

It's time to stop brooding and start blooming.

searching

searching
in the land
of scarcity
unrest
worries

not knowing how
not knowing where
not knowing what
not knowing who
not knowing when

your light is dimmed
and sometimes extinguished
you don't see it
you don't feel it
you don't believe it

you go with the flow
struggling to find your own way
in the busyness
of your thoughts
where is the emergency exit

setting boundaries
to yourself
to your thoughts
to your behavior
to your environment

yes your boundaries are set
still wobbly
in contact with yourself
in contact with others
you react from you

after a while
you see the effect of your movement
back in yourself
back in your behavior
back in the environment

even though it was sometimes hard
you are an example
for your environment
who respects and values you
your turn

follow the inspiration
the light is on
you are visible
to the people
who need your help

self-boundary

busy life
we talk a lot
about setting boundaries

with relationships
with work
with money

one boundary
we often forget
is with ourselves

it's time to be honest
to say "no" more often
not just to the world outside
but especially to yourself

as an entrepreneur you feel
what's good for others
you know what they need
but in that process you forget yourself

by not saying "no" to yourself
you shortchange yourself

we tolerate too much
things that are not good for us
we believe our own excuses
allow voices that keep us small

how can you set boundaries with others
if you don't respect your own boundaries
how can you help others
if you neglect yourself

it's time to shift focus
to your own needs your own desires

practice saying "no" to yourself
to thoughts you tolerate
to excuses
to the voice that holds you back

redefine your boundaries
not just with others
but especially with yourself

strengthen that self-boundary
so you can fully say "yes"
to your own growth and success

as a person you have the power
to empower yourself
to live from insight
to crush it with your own energy

discipel

become a disciple
of yourself
everything is in you
you are successful
all you have to do
is see it

we now live in a time
where we can no longer hide
life challenges us
to embrace
own truth
stand for who we are

a baby so pure and light
raised in systems and patterns
generations of survival
patterns hold us back
voices of others
seeking approval safety

you notice it doesn't work
you avoid, you please
the choice to do it differently
calls louder unrest grows chaos follows
the call to be yourself
grows stronger

you can no longer ignore it
you have to choose
not out of selfishness
not out of fear
but out of self-love
believe in yourself

you are the center of your growth
only then can you help others
become a disciple of your own belief
thank yourself daily
finding yourself

who are you already

who are you already?
the focus is outside you
on what you are not
can't do yet
where you're not yet
missed opportunities
dreamed qualities

who are you already?
focus inside you
what you already are
what you're good at
where you are now
achieved successes
your zone of genius

No one can be as unique ME as I am!

Words of thanks

Thank you, reader, for taking the time to read!

First and foremost, I want to express my deepest gratitude to the people closest to me—family and friends. Your unconditional support in everything I do gives me the strength and freedom to live life on my own terms. Without you, I wouldn't have been able to walk this path.

My sincere thanks also go to my spiritual coach Marion vdG and coaches Jesse Johnson, David Neagle, and Michael Neill. You have given me the courage to face the parts of myself that I preferred to avoid. Thanks to your guidance, I have gained new insights that have greatly enriched both my life and my work.

I am also deeply grateful to my clients, who have the courage to be so vulnerable. Your trust and openness allow me to gain profound insight into what's happening within you. Working with you has been a tremendous source of inspiration for me.

Finally, a special thanks to my daughters. You have grown into amazing people, and I am so proud of who you have become. Thank you for your encouragement, your calls when you face challenges, and simply for being who you are in my life.

About the author

Ivonne van Dis is a senior coach and business reader, and the expert in unraveling subconscious processes and achieving business success. With her combination of business acumen and personal advice, she helps executives and entrepreneurs find a better balance between their personal and professional lives.

In 2009, she started her own business, even though she didn't initially see herself as an entrepreneur. She struggled with applying her extensive knowledge in a structured way and found it difficult to make decisions. This battle between emotions and thoughts cost her a lot of energy, money, and time.

After completing a four-year Reader training program in 2013, she came to understand who she truly is and what was holding her back. By letting go of her need for control and learning to live in alignment with her true desires, her confidence and strength grew. This transformation led to a breakthrough in her entrepreneurial journey.

She has learned to critically examine her own thoughts and passes this insight on to her clients, helping them find greater happiness and success in both life and work. Her clients appreciate her relaxed approach to business and see her as a role model for running a business with ease.

Her mission is to help entrepreneurs reconnect with their true selves and their motivations, transforming this connection into business success. She believes that when these two elements are aligned, it leads to increased joy, motivation, and success, resulting in true freedom.

For more information, visit www.ivonnevandis.nl.
You can now chat to gain even more insights with the 'Reading Glasses for Thoughts' chatbot. Interested? Send an email to ivonne@ivonnevandis.nl